IT'S OK

A Personal Journey of Grief and Loss
and How to Overcome

By
Princess S. Millens

Copyright © 2021 by Princess S. Millens

All rights reserved. No part of this book may be used or reproduced by any means, graphic, electronic, or mechanical, including photocopying, recording, taping, or by any information storage retrieval system, without the written permission of the publisher except in the case of brief quotations embodied in critical articles and reviews.

HELP ME OUT PUBLICATIONS ™

DEDICATION

For my daughters, DeAndrea and Ayanna.

You both helped me to not get stuck in my sorrow and

I am so proud of you for overcoming your own journey of grief.

For all the readers of this book, don't give up!

You will get through this if you hang in there.

Table of Contents

Introduction 1

Chapter 1: In the Beginning 3

Chapter 2: I Will Never Forget 11

Chapter 3: The Waiting Period 18

Chapter 4: Welcome Home 24

Chapter 5: Gone, but Not Goodbye 33

Chapter 6: The Faces of Grief 38

Chapter 7: Learning to Journey through the Grief ... 45

A Prayer For You 53

Scriptures to Help You on Your Journey of Breakthrough 55

About The Author 58

Introduction

The journey of grief is hard! Yes, it is a journey. It is more than just going through some psychological steps; it is a process of feeling pain and processing the endless emotions that can come from it. Many people often find themselves in a process of grief that can be unrecognizable to the naked eye and does not fit the cookie-cutter idea of how many people may view grief. Grief has many faces: sadness, crying, anger, mood swings and the like, but very few people see grief in smiles, hard work, and doing life. We (the ones who grieve as well as those around us) must educate ourselves on these many faces so that it will not suffocate our lives and lead to hopelessness, addictions, suicide and much more.

I have experienced great losses in my life and there was a period of time where I believed that I would never get through it. Grief is a condition that no one can carry for you. You have to walk out the process for yourself. No one can ever give your grief an expiration date or tell you how to go through the process. Therefore, it is always necessary to find strategies that will help you continue to live. I must warn you - I am a born-again believer! I believe in God the Father, Jesus Christ the Son, and the Holy Spirit Divine. I mention this because I want to be clear upfront concerning what to expect in this book. My reliance on Jesus Christ is my strategy for overcoming grief. He has kept and sustained me through it all and I am unapologetically grateful for His faithfulness towards me.

Grief has been and continues to be a journey that I travel. Somehow it becomes a part of you, just like another part of your body. However, it is through grief that we learn our strengths and weaknesses. In this book, you will receive principles and guided instruction to help you navigate through the pain and process of grief. It is something that you have to constantly work on daily so that you do not slip further into a place of darkness and hopelessness. It is my prayer that when you read these pages, that you will obtain divine revelation that will help you overcome and gain wisdom on how to move forward in life. May your heart be stirred and encouraged that you can be an overcomer as well!

Chapter 1

In the Beginning

Grief is a journey that goes through a process of pain, expectations, and revelations about the life that was and the life that is. My life before this journey began somewhat simple. I was born and raised in a Christian home, the youngest of four siblings. I grew up in the church and began to learn more and more about Jesus Christ. My mom was a church musician and through her I learned the importance of worship. I used to hear the deacons start every service with prayer. I remember thinking that one day I would know how to pray also. This upbringing was something that I have always held on to, and made it a significant part of my life.

Understandably, life became more complex as I got older. I got married and I had my first daughter in my late 20s. After her birth, I became depressed. I began to always worry about my daughter: is she okay? What if something is wrong and I don't know? Can I protect her properly? Many irrational thoughts began to surface. Little did I know that it was postpartum depression.

Even though I had lived most of my life going to church, I didn't learn how to effectively pray. I did not know how to pray myself out of the depression, but I could only say "God help me". Over time that seemed to be enough. What I have learned over the years is that God hears our prayers even when they are small. I know that God heard me because I was able to finally be free from postpartum depression.

I lived my early adulthood with little preparation or thought about the future. Not because I didn't know how, but because I was just not interested in long-term goals. Even when I started a family, I never really made plans. I had mostly stopped going to church for several years by then and really had a lack of prayer in my life. Prayer was not routine; it had become something that I did only when tough times came.

However, I had a friend who invited me to church. It was then that I embarked on a new journey to become solid in the knowledge of God and to learn to pray. I learned a lot during this time and began to work in the church with the youth ministry programs and other committees. I was able to take my children to church so that they also could have a foundation in Christ Jesus. They were baptized, we were all learning and serving together, and life was good. However, my prayer life still did not totally develop. I did not place emphasis on digging deeper and continued to go through life spending most of my prayers when I needed something from God.

The fact of the matter is that I had experienced loss and grief before. I left the church in late 2003, my marriage was very unstable, and ultimately it came to an end. One of my biggest pains was when my mother passed away in December 2004. She was gone very quickly. She went into the hospital in November right before Thanksgiving and she was gone the week before Christmas.

That loss was very hard for me, primarily because I saw my mom deteriorate before my eyes in those few weeks. She was not the vibrant person that I had known. The hospital referred her to hospice, however, she just wanted to come home and we obeyed her wishes. Her last word to me was that she loved me, which was about 4 days before she died. When I arrived to see her that day, the nurse had already given her morphine and she was seemingly in a deep coma-like sleep. I knew that she was in there and somehow that she could hear me. So, I began to talk to her. I let her know that we (her children) would be okay, and it was okay if she had to go. I didn't know what I was saying because I was certainly not ready for the inevitable.

I remember speaking on the phone with someone saying that she wasn't going to make it. However, at the same time I was pleading in my heart for God to save her. I didn't really know how to pray back then, and was not surrounded by anyone who had a prayer life. A few hours later, I was there holding my mom while she was taking her last breath. I felt her spirit leave her body and I was consumed with grief. My best friend was gone, and I felt lost in the world. My mom always knew what to say in any situation that I asked her for help. However, I believe that this is one of the events in my life that ultimately began my new journey to seek answers and strategies from heaven.

Years later after my mother's transition, I found myself in the same place with prayer: I did not understand the power of prayer and didn't know the strategies for an effective prayer life. I even began to think that maybe if I knew how to pray my mother would still be here, or my life would be happier, or that I would not have lost all of the things that I had lost in life, or perhaps if I knew how to pray, I would not have made some of the decisions in life that were counterproductive. But I certainly had not yet found the scripture Romans 8:28!

"And we know that all things work together for good to those who love God, to those who are the called according to *His* purpose." Yet I was still not in a place where I was actively seeking to get back to church and grow deeper in God. However, I believe that God always knows what we need in the time that we need it. So, after about 10 years, I received another invitation to church. It was the beginning of my journey to an effective prayer life.

As I began to embed myself back in the church, my thoughts were to only be a professional parishioner: one who just goes to church, loves to praise and worship, to learn more about Christ, how to pray and how to apply it to my life, and go home and put it into action. In retrospect, it was a selfish desire because it never occurred to me that I could have a spiritual impact on someone else's life. I had always left that to the pastors and others in the five-fold ministry.

However, I began to see and do more. Not only did I attend Sunday services, but I attended bible studies and prayer meetings, and participated more in the prayer ministry of the church. I began to listen and learn from the elders who were teaching God's word and praying. They began to give me opportunities to pray and get stronger in faith. I began to develop into a woman of prayer. I was hungry and thirsty for God and I wanted a better life in Christ, as I had desired from the beginning. It was finally happening because I was finally settled, and I evolved before my own eyes. I became the leader in the prayer ministry and a leader in the church. I began to excel in my career and education. My children became strengthened by seeing me mature in the faith and they began to learn to pray and read the Word of God as well.

These are results that I did not seek after but happened as a result of my steadfastness and dedication to the things of God. We all have this same opportunity! If we want a better life, if we want to know how to pray, if we want to go deeper in God's Word, then we must surround ourselves with the people who are already doing these things.

God gave me the community of believers that helped to transform my life, but I had to be diligent to take advantage of what was before me. Sometimes, God will give us exactly what we need, but we will miss the blessing and opportunity because we don't know how to use what He has given. This had been my missing ingredient all these years. I had never surrounded myself with people whose lives were devoted to prayer at this level. Because I really didn't know how to pray, it never occurred to me to ask God for this in my life. This is what prayer can do: it can lead you to ask God for the things that you don't even know that you need! And He will deliver on His promises every single time.

To help you overcome the trials of life, you must find yourself in a ministry of prayer! Before loss and grief struck my life, I was a person that was just wading through life. A stronger prayer life gave me the intimate access and communication with God that I long desired. It allowed me to be able to not only pray for myself, but intercede effectively for others. It gave me a newfound hope for my children to have the courage to get closer to God and desire Him more.

More importantly, it gave me a covering and the faith that I would need later to conquer one of the most painful events in my life: the death of my son, Anthony. Life will never be perfect, but Prayer is able to keep me coming to a place of stability in life. Even when I got down, I was never out, because prayer pushed me right back up. Little did I know then that what I was to endure later in my life, I would need prayer all the more. Prayer is powerful in transition! I pray that God places you in a community of prayer warriors and I encourage you to keep praying in the good times and the bad times.

Chapter 2

I Will Never Forget

It was a normal day for me. I went to school. I was in my classroom teaching. I teach high school math, 10th grade. It was around 9:45 am and I was in second period. My daughter and her friend showed up at my door and I saw them through the glass opening. They've done that before, come to see me at school. So, I was not alarmed and was happy to see them. I came out of the room to greet them and she explained that her dad said to come get me from school and bring me home. I asked, "What's going on?" She replied, "I don't know what's going on. You know, he just said, Go get your mom. Bring her home."

At that point, my daughter started crying and I started crying too. I began thinking that it was something to do with my dad. My dad was 75 years old and had health issues in the past. However, I never thought that it could be any of my children. Thankfully, the school secretary was there as she was the one who escorted my daughter to my room. I had some friends across the hall that could cover my class until a substitute could be secured. I quickly packed my belongings and left with my daughter.

As we drove home, we had a normal conversation and I began doing what we normally do when we are trying to see what is going on: we start calling each other. I actually didn't call Anthony, I texted him. I can't even remember what I said but I am sure that I asked if he was alright. Anthony was in the military, stationed at Ft. Bliss, Texas. Due to the nature of his job, I did not expect an immediate answer. My daughter was driving and I was texting my son. Little did I know then that my daughter had already tried to contact him herself.

We finally got home and Anthony's dad was there next to the driveway, sitting in the car. I got out of the car and went to his car to see what was happening. I could tell that he had been crying. At the exact time that I opened my mouth to ask what was happening, there was a car driving down our street which stopped at my mailbox. Two military men exited their car and began walking toward me. I had seen enough movies to know that they were not there for good news. As they approached me, I began walking down the street in the opposite direction, praying to God to not allow this to be true. I began screaming to the top of my lungs "God, please!" I was begging God, please God let this be a dream. My worst fears were happening right before my eyes. Something that I could have never fathomed in my mind. Those fears in my heart began to seep out in my prayers as I was walking down that street. As fear began to grip me, I began praying to God to save my son. To not let me have to bury my son. And to even question God, why didn't He just take me? Fear overshadowed me and I did not know what to do. Anthony's dad came down the street to get me. I remember saying, "I cannot do this". He said, "Yes, we must and we will". I kept saying that I can't, I just can't. All of this happened even before the military officers said a word.

It's just like the movies. When the people get out the car dressed in their military Class A uniforms. So when I saw them, my head knew what was going on, but my heart could not catch up. I knew that they were not coming for good news. They had come to my house early that morning, but I was already at work and nobody was home. When they could not reach me at home, they went to Anthony's dad's house. So actually, he was the one that received the news first.

A short while later, after I found the strength to face the officers, I walked back to the house. The officers came into the house and, as you would imagine, spoke those horrifying words that they were sorry to inform me about the passing of my son, Private Anthony Freeman. I cringed when I heard those words, but still somehow in my heart refused to believe it. I wanted to know what happened, but they had no clear answers, only that he had passed away in his sleep.

They gave me some paperwork to sign regarding their visit and what my next steps should be as I prepared for my son to come home. Everything is protocol with the military and they gave us some information about who I would need to contact. I was assigned a casualty officer who was to be my contact with the military to take care of anything that I needed regarding Anthony's case and provide updates for any developing information.

After the military officers left my home, it was just a period of time where we (me, Anthony's dad, and my daughter and friend) were outside in the yard trying to comprehend what had just taken place. I was literally in such a fog. I didn't know what to do or who to call. I urged them to tell others not to place any information on social media because my youngest daughter was still at school in Albany and she did not know what happened.

We quickly made a plan to go get her. In the meantime, I remember just calling my dad, my brother, and my pastor. I didn't know what to say and remember stumbling for words. It probably took me about 10 seconds to even say something when I called them on the phone and the words wouldn't even come out. However, once the words came, the tears came again. It felt like it was all such a horrible dream.

As I begin to think about that day, I remember that I prayed for God to not take my son away. As I received this heartbreaking news, fear began to grip my heart and was released through my prayer. I was begging God to allow me to wake up from this nightmare and that all would be well with my son. The overshadowing of fear in this situation caused me to pray from my soul and not from my spirit. I could only see what I wanted and not what God had already done. I was blinded by the fear of thinking about what my life was going to be like without my son, and the hurt that was already in my heart. Prayers that are released from the foundation of fear is not God's intention for prayer. God's mind is that He did not give us the spirit of fear, but of power, love, and a sound mind (2 Timothy 1:7).

Instead of saying "I can't do this" I could have prayed, "I can do all things through Christ who strengthens me". Yes, even in death and grief, we give God's word back to Him. It is hard to remember this sometimes when your flesh is caught off guard or weak. However, know that God always hears our hearts and prayers, even before we speak them.

We must give everything to Him in our prayers because He is the only one who has the answers. The answers may not be in line with what we want, but God is Sovereign and His will shall be done on the earth. Therefore, we must always ask God for the strength and heart to accept His will, no matter what.

Chapter 3

The Waiting Period

The waiting period between being notified about Anthony's death and actually having him home was emotionally loaded. It was a week before Anthony would come home. The military officials did not release him to me until they had completed an autopsy. It would take at least 3 days, and then an order would have to be signed to fly him back home. They told me that they were going to do an autopsy because he was young with no real health issues and he had passed away in his sleep. They, as well as I, wanted to see what happened. So they stated that it would take about three or four days to complete it.

They ordered the autopsy but they had to order him to be released back to me when they were done. He was coming from Ft. Bliss, Texas, where he was stationed as a motor transport operator (88M). Meanwhile, I had to decide if I wanted them to prepare him for burial prior to his return, which is what I chose to do. Therefore, when he came home, there would be no delay and it was ensured that he would be dressed properly in his military attire.

During this waiting period, I was going through the motions, because part of me still did not believe it was true. I was advised to go ahead and notify the funeral home that would receive Anthony when he arrived. I began making arrangements on Friday by visiting neighboring funeral homes and trying to wrap my mind around what was happening. I went to about three funeral homes, but still, in my mind, it was just surreal because I ended up thinking, "I don't believe this is happening, I don't believe that I'm doing this." Imagine going to these funeral homes and saying, "I'm trying to make arrangements for my son who I haven't seen!" I think that my heart was still holding out for a chance that it could be a mistake.

Visitors began coming to the house on the Saturday and Sunday after I received the news. My casualty officer visited on that Saturday morning with some preliminary information. It was very difficult to have that meeting to discuss the deceased son that I had not seen. Some of the information that he was sharing was noisy, because I was silently talking to God. I was sharing my heart with Him and saying how painful this was. I was also asking God, could this be a mistake? Could it be that it is some horrific identity mix-up? I was trying to rationalize everything to God. What I have learned is that it is always okay to talk to God. He wants to hear from us every day, whether in good times or bad times. It is our close and intimate experiences with God that help us to process pain. It may not be immediate, but it begins the process of healing.

After the officer left, visitors began arriving… with LOTS of food. There were many encouraging words and conversations from everyone. Members of my prayer ministry came to visit throughout the weekend. They filled my home with prayer and worship, which continued my own worship to God. Our prayers of sorrow changed to prayers of praise and thanksgiving. God filled my home with His presence as more people began to arrive. Many may wonder, how could a mother who just lost her child praise God? The simple answer is that scripture tells us to rejoice, pray without ceasing, and give thanks in all things because it is God's will for us. This tells us that we should have an attitude of joy, thanksgiving, and prayer no matter the circumstances. Well, how can I do this for my only son? My heart had already been postured to a life of praise, worship, and prayer. I began to think about all of the blessings that God had given me and everything that He has done for me in life. I began to thank God for the blessings. I told God that even though my heart was hurting, I would still give Him the praise and honor that

He deserves. Also, I began to ask God to help me deal with the pain and to show me how to make it through that trying time. Even though God is omniscient, I still needed Him to hear me; He still wants to hear from us as well. He knows what things we are in need of even before we ask. I knew that I would need His help to endure such pain. My prayers reflected this request, as well as to let Him know that I still claim Him Lord over my life. To display that type of strength, I had to pull on the strength of the foundation of prayer that God had already helped me to establish so that I could press through the pain.

It's Ok to Cry

As I continued to wait day-by-day to receive Anthony home, I continued to bounce back and forth with the resulting emotions of the news of his death. I was given this news, but somehow I still could not wrap my mind and heart around the fact that he was gone. After all, I still had not seen him. In the days after all of the guests left, I continued to wonder and ask God if this was a horrible mistake. I remembered the days when Anthony would have to do work in the field and would be unreachable by phone or text for a few days. I began to rationalize in my mind of all the reasons why this could be a mistake. I continued to talk to God and plead with Him to not let this be real.

God didn't say much to me as I rehearsed the possible scenarios, but I know that He heard my every word. How do I know? I know because I did not lose my mind and continued to ask God for His strength. Even with all of the doubts and hurts, God heard my cries for emotional stability. There is always power in talking to God because He is a great listener and cares about all that concerns us. We may not receive the answer that we want, but He is there to comfort us along the way.

A few days later, I received a call informing me that he would finally be coming home and to prepare to meet him at the airport. My casualty officer set everything up and gave me the details of Anthony's arrival. I was closer to seeing the truth with my own eyes. The truth that I did not want to see. Reality was about to hit me over the head and I was not ready. Therefore, I continued to do only what I know how to do… PRAY.

I prayed that God would continue to strengthen me and comfort my heart. I prayed that God would settle my heart and emotions. My prayers were heard and God gave me what I asked. God can always see the hearts of His children, and my heart was broken. He heard my prayers because my heart continued to be open toward Him, for Him to provide everything that I needed. When our heart is clean and open during our prayers, God will move mightily on our behalf. I thank God for hearing me because I would need everything that I asked in the days to come, even as I need it today.

Chapter 4

WELCOME HOME

The day that I would greet Anthony home had arrived and I didn't know what to expect. When the military escorts your loved one back home, the family may go to the airport to receive them home. On the day that Anthony came home, my casualty officers and team from Fort Gordon in Augusta, Georgia were present as well. Military protocol has established that someone from the departure will escort your loved one back home, and then there is an exchange to the receiving officers in the home state, and ultimately to the family.

Although we were scheduled to be at the airport at 7pm, there was an hour delay in Anthony's arrival. So as we (my daughters, their dad, my dad, and I) anxiously awaited for my son to arrive in Atlanta, we were in a waiting area very near the plane's landing area. We passed most of the time with small talk, however my heart and mind was never really in the conversation. I was focused on the slow-moving reality that this nightmare must be real. I do not know why my heart continued to bargain with God, even at this late stage of being told about the passing of my son. However, I continued to beg God not to let this be reality. I wanted Him to wake me up from this never-ending nightmare. I wanted Him to tell me that this was all a big mistake. I wanted my heart to stop hurting.

The officer came to tell us that it would be about 15 minutes before we could go back to the receiving area. Fifteen more minutes! Well, I did the only thing I knew how to do… I prayed. I led the family in prayer. I thanked God for keeping us and covering our minds. I thanked God that He gave us the grace to be here. I praised God for all that He had done to sustain us during this time. Further, I asked God to give us the strength to be able to receive Anthony home with dignity. It is important that when we pray that we not only thank God for what He has done, but also thank Him in advance for getting us through the next stage in our situations in life. I knew that without God, I would not have the strength to endure. I asked God for exactly what I needed. When your heart is open to God, He even gives you the things that you don't know you need.

I am sure that I needed more than strength, I needed Him to equip me with whatever I needed. If you place everything in God's hands through thanksgiving and prayer, you will always have everything that you need to persevere.

That 15 minutes seemed like an hour. The plane had already touched down, but the military protocol of escorting and receiving had to be done in order. We were finally brought back to the area where Anthony would come off the plane. We did not see the actual plane but were in the receiving area. The funeral home personnel were there as well, having assumed their position to take Anthony to the funeral home. All of the military officers who had traveled from Augusta had taken their respective place in formation.

The airport workers had also gathered in their respective areas as they prepared to bring Anthony off the plane. We all sat nervously for another several minutes as my casualty officer explained to me what was about to take place and what the family could do once they ushered Anthony off the plane. He walked back to the receiving point to take his place in the ceremony. Finally, after a silence that lasted a few minutes, we saw the flag draped casket being slowly driven into the building. As they took the casket out of the vehicle, my heart began to sink all over again. The officers began to roll the casket to a designated spot in the center of the building.

This is the point when we could go up and do whatever we needed to do; however, we could not open the casket. I continued to sit for several seconds, but was the first to go up to the casket. I began to drape my arms around the casket, calling my son's name with a screeching sound. Then, as the rest of the family was coming up, I began to do again what only I know how to do… Pray.

It wasn't a prayer like God, why did you do this? It was a prayer like, God, I just thank you. Thank you for showing him purpose in his life. I began thanking God for not letting him suffer. I thanked God for giving me Anthony and for the service that he had given his country. I began to tell God that I did not understand why this was happening but that I trusted Him even in my lack of understanding. I began to even pray for the officers that were present to escort my son home and the ones that were there to receive him home. I start thanking God for everybody who was there who were just so helpful and so compassionate. I prayed that God would continue to strengthen them and give them courage to keep serving. I prayed for the airport staff and their emotional and mental health as they saw so many soldiers come home the same way that Anthony did. Most importantly, I began to pray for my family, especially my daughters. That they would not be mad at God and blame Him for allowing this to happen. I prayed that they would continue to be built up in the most holy faith and continue to trust God in all things.

My prayers progressed from faith, to thanksgiving, and then intercession. I am sure that many people were bewildered about how I could pray for others at a time like this. I have learned that in all things, give thanks. It is not that you are not going to have hard times or times of suffering, but you should always give praise and thanks to God for being with you every step of the way.

After we spent our time receiving Anthony home, there was a processional of everyone escorting Anthony to the funeral home. Once we arrived, the military officers proceeded with the small ceremony to take Anthony into the chapel. As we stood and watched, my heart was still sinking because I still could not believe that this was happening. As they placed Anthony in the chapel, they only allowed his dad and I to go into the chapel to take as long as we needed. However, we still could not open the casket. I still could not see him until it was approved by the receiving funeral home a couple of days later. It was protocol that the receiving funeral home had to inspect him first before opening him to us. It would take them 24 hours to get him ready and we could finally see him after that time.

I was apprehensive for those two days, but I continued to ask God for the strength to endure. When Anthony's dad and I finally arrived at the funeral home 2 days later, I knew that this would be the moment of truth. The time that I would finally see for myself what everyone has been saying: my son is really dead. I prepared myself to go into the parlor and there he laid, so peaceful as if he was asleep. My eyes immediately welled with tears and with the reality that he was really gone. I suddenly remembered the tattoo that Anthony had shown me on his arm. His entire arm from shoulder to wrist was covered with the scripture of Proverbs 3 verses 5 through 6: "Trust in the Lord with all your heart,

And lean not on your own understanding; In all your ways acknowledge Him, And He shall direct your paths." Can you imagine that? His entire arm held this scripture. I do not know why he chose that scripture, however, I know that during his military career there would be things that he did not understand or may have made him afraid. Therefore, to trust God is the only thing that we can do in order to allow God to be the center of every situation and help us each day in life.

As I remembered the scripture that was now covered by his military uniform, it began to hold a special place in my heart to guide my journey of grief and the intercession that would follow. I began to do once again that only thing that I knew how to do… talk to God about it in prayer. As I laid my hands on Anthony's hands, I once again began to thank God for allowing me to be his mother and to see what great things that he did in life. I began to tell God that I did not understand why this was happening, but to help me to trust with all of my heart. I began to even thank God for the funeral home directors, who had made this difficult time bearable with the compassion and kindness they showed each day. Finally, I began to thank God for allowing me to remember the tattoo.

The tattoo represents to me that my son saw his mother as a woman of God's word and prayer. I was not just another preacher to him. He had noticed my transformation to becoming a woman of prayer and a lover of God's word, and it began to penetrate his heart as well. God allowed me to see something. I have always prayed that my children would have a personal relationship with Jesus Christ. Even though they didn't go to church often, I still wanted them to know who God is and know how to pray for themselves. It was comforting to me to know that, so when I saw him, and I remembered that tattoo, I also began to thank God that Anthony knew Him before he closed his eyes to eternal sleep.

It is very important to train your children, even when they seem rebellious. They may respond to what you say, but they will always remember what you do. Proverbs 22:6 says to "Train up a child in the way he should go, And when he is old he will not depart from it." Anthony was the average teenager; still exploring the world for himself and sometimes getting in trouble for it at home. I saw him change as I began to get stronger in the Word and prayer. God allowed me to see the change in him before he died, and I am so grateful.

Proverbs 3:5-6 is the scripture that Anthony stood on each day and it has become a key scripture that has guided my journey through the pain of grief and loss. Prayers of thanksgiving are a weapon. In the midst of pain, I created prayers of thanksgiving. I began covering my family in prayer that they would be protected from the pain so they wouldn't give up on God. I desired for God to protect the emotional wellbeing of me and my family and that is exactly what He began to do.

Chapter 5

Gone, but Not Goodbye

The funeral was the first Wednesday in November 2018, the day after election day. On the day prior, we had a family visitation at the funeral home. It was tough being there, but there was such an outpouring of love with people young and old, family and friends coming to pay their respects to Anthony. It was the first collective glance that I had of how Anthony's life touched so many.

Before the immediate family arrived, there were so many people who had already visited and signed the memorial book. I was deeply moved by the outpouring of love and support, but it would never be enough to soothe my heart of all of the hurt and pain that I was experiencing at that time. As my pastor closed the gathering in prayer, my heart prayed along silently with him and I began to thank God for the love and support shown by my family and friends. No matter where you are, whether audible or not, prayer is always the best response to a broken heart.

It's Ok to Cry

We gathered for the funeral the next day. My dad and I rode in a funeral car alone together, not speaking a word but it was very symbolic. My brother passed away before I was born. He was only 2 years old. I can only imagine the pain that my parents felt back then. I remember when I was a teenager my mom spoke briefly to me about the pain of losing my brother; it was clear that even nearly 20 years later it was still a deep-seeded pain in her life. It was the pain that I would have to endure now. My dad spoke volumes to me even without saying a word in that car. My mother was not there physically for words of comfort, but my dad knew exactly what I was going through. He is not a man of many words, but I began to thank God for my dad being there for me that day.

As the funeral service was near to an end, I stood before the people to say thanks for all of the love and support shown. With my words of thanks, I briefly described Anthony as a brave and courageous son who did not meet a stranger. The one with the big heart that would do anything for his family and friends. As I stood there talking, I began to pray. I thanked God for giving me such an awesome son and allowing me to be his mother. I thanked God for making room for him in heaven and giving him a seat at His table. As I continued to thank God for giving Anthony to me, I gave Anthony back to Him. His work here on earth was done and he had done it well. With my prayers, I made an appeal to the people to not cry tears of sadness and leave that funeral with the same heart. I wanted everyone to know that there was still time to live right, to love right, to serve right, to forgive, and make things right with others.

My prayers of thanksgiving turned to supplication that no one else would die and not receive the gift of salvation and/or be at odds with their family or friends. Problem is, you never know when it will be your last day to tell someone you love them, or to apologize to someone that you have wronged. I wanted them to know that their life is valuable and people are always watching. People were watching Anthony, and you could tell by the attendance of his funeral and memorial services, and the wonderful memories that were shared by so many.

The military planned a memorial service for Anthony during the week of Thanksgiving 2018. At the ceremony, they had the flags, his boots, his helmet, his M-16 rifle, his military dog tags, a wreath, and Anthony's picture. At his feet, many of the soldiers at Ft. Bliss had left symbols of their friendship and respect for a fellow fallen soldier. As we entered the auditorium, they were playing the video of memories of Anthony that I did not get to play at the funeral. There were hundreds of soldiers in attendance to pay their respects. At the end of the ceremony, the family got a chance to go up to the memorial display to have some time to ourselves. I went up first, then his dad and sisters followed. It was very difficult for all of us because it was as if we had lost him all over again. The tears filled our eyes once more and I could not wait to get back to the reception area where we had waited for the ceremony to begin. They left us in the room to have a moment.

Again I did what only I know how when my heart is full… I prayed. I continued to pray for our hearts and that God would heal our family of grief. I prayed that Anthony's life would be a testimony to many that they could too trust in the Lord with all their hearts. I began to intercede for the soldiers there in Ft. Bliss. I thanked God for their lives and all that they do to keep our country safe. I asked God to continue to protect them and bless them. These are similar prayers that I had prayed before, but I realized that God hears your voice, but He also hears your heart. We should never be overly concerned with praying the same thing to God.

We may have to go to God in prayer for the same request and that is okay. I felt like I was burying my son all over again and I needed to talk to God about it. He loves when we share our heart with Him and take time with Him. Yes, God already knows. He is omniscient. However, He desires a true relationship with His children and prayer is a large aspect of that relationship. My way out of the bondage of grief has always been prayer, not only for myself and family, but interceding for others, even when I needed prayer for myself. Prayer takes the focus off the problem and places the focus on the Problem Solver, our Almighty God, where perfect peace is ultimately found. With Him all things are possible and I know that His promise to be close to the brokenhearted is real, and prayer was the vehicle that helped me to remain in His presence.

Chapter 6

THE FACES OF GRIEF

There are many faces of grief and we all grieve differently. Pain looks different on everyone. Some people stay in bed and never leave the house, while others go from day to day trying to be 'normal'. It may look like a person over or undereating. Perhaps they are exercising too much; all of this to cover up the pain and hurt. Maybe their attitude has changed to dark and negative thoughts. There are similarities and differences and there is no right or wrong way to grieve. However, we all must do the work to journey through the process. That work for me always began and ended with prayer.

Grief can begin with denial. Denial is present when you cannot bring yourself to believe that your loved one is gone. Denial was my first face of grief. Even though everyone around me was saying that Anthony had transitioned, mentally I was denying that this was true, especially during the waiting period before I saw him for the first time. The pain of grief can be displayed in different ways. However, sometimes pain doesn't look like pain. I was going to work, I continued to serve in the church. Still smiling, just heartbroken. I got the news about Anthony on Thursday, October 25, 2018. However, I went back to work Monday. For two days, I stood before my students and taught them Geometry as my heart was still breaking.

I couldn't believe it and I'm sure that my students didn't either. I thought I was in grief at the time that I received the news about Anthony and I was in a broad sense, but really not. I was in shock and just surviving. I know that I was sustained through the strength of God and my prayers. After those two days of being at work, I stayed home for nearly two weeks until after the funeral. What I understand now is that grief sometimes comes later... After the funeral, after everyone goes home, after everyone stops calling every day. When you are forced to be alone with only you and God, your thoughts, and your emotions.

Perhaps the pain was greater for me, because the holiday season was beginning. Thanksgiving was approaching, a time we had set aside for simple family togetherness. But this year, we were missing Anthony, the jokester, the one who could bring joy to any situation. I remember in 2015, Anthony, the girls, and I started contributing to the holiday meal by making a personalized dish. We had a tradition of everybody making a dish for Thanksgiving and for Christmas. Anthony, the non-cook, had to cook and got a chance to participate as well. Understandably, it was just different the Thanksgiving of 2018 because he was no longer here. Even after that, it looked to others as if I was alright.

Another face of grief is the anxiety and depression that are sometimes hidden. There were many days where I just wanted to not get out of the bed and pull the covers over my head and stay there. I was devastatingly heartbroken but good at camouflaging the hurt. How do I know that I was good? Because everyone who saw me only commended me for being so strong and resilient. They did not see the deep hurt behind my smiling eyes or feel the broken heart behind my words. Some people may try to condemn us for doing this. They will say, "Why didn't you reach out?" or "You could've called me," which is all true. However, depression is overwhelming and can give you the perspective that you do not want to burden others with your problems.

Many people do not see it unless you speak up and tell them, then there are others who can detect that something is wrong, even if you are smiling. Grief can make you fearful of crying in public. I never wanted others to see me crying after the funeral, even my daughters. I would hold it in and cry when they were asleep or any chance I got to be alone. I would cry in the car after church or work. I would cry in my classroom during times when my students were not present. It was especially important to me that I did not cry in front of my daughters because I never wanted them to worry about me. Depression is a lonely place. You can be in a room full of people and still feel alone in your grief. Loneliness may cause you to reach out to other things, anything, that will help ease the pain. Many people may turn to alcohol, drug use, or sex in an attempt to not feel so alone with their grief. However, people or things will never replace your loss and is not an easy fix to loneliness. I realized through it all that all of these emotions were normal, but I knew that I could not remain in that emotional state of mind.

Grief can also have the face of guilt, which is to have a perspective that the loss is somehow our fault. I began to think and rationalize with God that maybe his death was my fault. Perhaps I didn't do enough or maybe I didn't pray enough for Anthony. I began to ask God what I did wrong. I remember promising Anthony that I would come to Ft. Bliss to visit him. I didn't get a chance to and then he was off to his deployment to Poland.

He remained in Poland for about 9 months and came to visit me about a month before his death. I thought that I had time to go meet his friends and see the life that he had made in Texas and I never did. The guilt began to overwhelm me. I remember even during that time praying to God about this guilt that I was feeling. I remember that I began to talk to Anthony as if he was there in the room with me. I remember saying, "Anthony, I'm sorry, I'm sorry. I'm so sorry. I didn't come. I'm sorry if I didn't pray. I'm sorry if I disappointed you by not keeping my promise." Even though I was praying and sharing my heart with God, I just wanted to release the guilt from my heart by telling him I was sorry.

After the week of Thanksgiving, I was called to jury duty. I had hoped that I would not be selected, but I was the first name that was called and I was selected for a case! The case lasted only one week and once again my aim was to act as normal as possible. No one there knew me and I could easily pretend. My heart was still breaking but I was determined to make it through the week. I remember meeting a woman there who had lost her son in the prior year from gun violence. She was very vocal about not trusting the police because of how her case was handled. Needless to say, she was not selected for the jury, however, I was compelled to speak to her before she left the courthouse. I mustered up the confidence and I began to give her my condolences regarding her son. I told her that I was also a mother who had recently lost her son. We spoke for a few moments, exchanged phone numbers, and embraced with a hug. I began to pray for her because it was evident that she was bitter about how her son died and the response that she had received from investigators. I knew then that my call for jury duty was much more than met the eye. God placed me in the place where a mother like me would need prayer. Her heart was not settled. Mine was not either, but I knew that prayer is the key to a settled mind and heart.

Our prayers for others have the power to bring peace to our lives as well, even in grief. I prayed that God would give her peace beyond her understanding. I asked God to help her to let go of the anger that she felt and fill her heart with forgiveness. I asked God to strengthen the family and friends around her to be able to support her when she needed it. I prayed for her when I needed prayer for myself. God makes no mistakes, and I was thankful that God chose me that day to speak to the heart of another mother whose heart was filled with grief. Remember, you do not have to be tormented by the pain. You can reach out to your family and friends. You can find a grief support group in your area. Most importantly, you can make prayer a lifestyle to release all the negative things in your heart and embrace peace, healing, and the overwhelming love of God.

Chapter 7

Learning to Journey through the Grief

Overcoming grief was a part of life for me. Even losing my mom, who was truly my best friend, back in 2004, and my grandmothers only months apart. What I have found is that many people who battle with grief haven't learned how to release the pain but at the same time keep the precious memory of their loved one. This is what happened to me. Sometimes you really believe that you are further along in the journey, but later realize that you hadn't released the pain at all; you only hid it from others as well as yourself. We can do this unknowingly, until we are triggered by something in life that reminds us of the pain.

At Anthony's funeral service, I stood to make remarks of thanks and began praying. I remember praying to thank God for giving me a son whom I loved and I prayed to release him back to God. I declared that Anthony was His and was His all the time. God was just gracious enough to allow me to borrow him and steward over Anthony's life. I remember thanking God for preparing that eternal table for my son receiving Him into eternity. I courageously prayed that prayer and I thought that I had truly released him.

A few months later in my prayer time, I began feeling guilty again about some promises that I made to Anthony that I did not have a chance to fulfill. I started praying and just began to talk to Anthony as if he was in the room. My eyes and heart flooded with tears and I felt the same way as the day I was given the news of his transition. I thought that I was handling it well, and I was.

]Everyone kept saying how strong I was and that it was an inspiration to them. However, I learned that day that I really had not totally released him. There was a part of me that continued to hang on as if he was coming back. The silver lining in it all is that God had already prepared me for this time in life. I was only "strong" because my God is strong and made perfect in my weakness. I had learned to pray my way through some things. I had learned to trust God even when I didn't understand. It was never me that people saw; it was the God in me that was sustaining me through this difficult time. Even during this time, there were times that I wanted to give up. I wanted to go back to a life that I lived long before to get myself through pain. I wanted to start back drinking the pain away and fornicating, because alcohol and sex always made me "feel better" so many years ago. I even wanted to end my life. I had contemplated and planned how I would do it.

What am I saying? Even in my "strength" I thought about these things because I continued to do everything to cover my pain to others, even my family. I was truly thankful that God received my son home and I often thought about the good memories that Anthony shared with everyone. None of that was an act. I continued to go to work, do ministry, and smile with the deep-seeded hurt and pain that was still present that I didn't know was there. Yet I never stopped praying, I never stopped believing that it would get better. Through it all, I have always been thankful to God for being faithful and sustaining my life.

So how do you release the pain in your heart and begin to overcome the loss? Could it be that you truly don't overcome grief? The key is to learn how to live better. Learn how to turn the sadness of the death and loss into the joy of the memories that are left with you. Grief is a path that takes us through a journey that we may not feel that we can overcome. I don't think anyone will ever "arrive". You never get over it, not really. Your heart is always going to miss them. Your heart is always going to want them here. This is what I say to myself; that I know I can live better, and I know that he would want me to live better. Anthony wouldn't want me to live in a state of grief or stop living. Therefore, how you overcome it is to just learn how to live better.

What is living better? Living better means getting back to the purpose and the plan that God has for your life. I had to put my focus back on the reason that God created me. Anthony had lived his life and fulfilled his purpose, no matter how short the span of life. His work was done. I saw hundreds of people that attended Anthony's funeral and memorial service and shared the same message: that he was such a giver and showed so many the character of genuine friendship. He served his country with pride and led a life of integrity and good character. I began to reflect on the legacy that I desire to leave behind. What did I want people to remember about me when I am gone? I concluded that I want to die empty. God has filled you and I with purpose and whatever He has placed in us, there should be nothing left to give when He calls us to heaven.

Living better meant that I had to remain in prayer and in God's word. Prayers of thanksgiving and seeing God in the good and bad times because He makes all things work together for our good. So, for my journey in overcoming grief, I remained active at my job and in ministry. I continued to pour into my students and others even when I needed it for myself. I continued to build programs to sow into the community. Life will certainly not be the same or as normal, but life doesn't have to be over. It becomes a new normal. The day will come when you're not crying daily anymore. You begin to receive joy back into your heart. It doesn't mean that you forget or don't miss your loved one, but your heart chooses joy over the pain.

It's Ok to Cry

It has been said that our loved ones die twice: once when breath leaves their body and lastly when their name is mentioned for the final time. However, I have come to understand that as our loved ones are no longer here physically, they will continue to live on through their legacy and when we continue to say their name. My son left a legacy of giving.

My daughters and I created the Anthony's Army foundation, which currently provides veterans with hats and motivational bracelets. My son loved hats and shoes and had so many in his wardrobe. We married his giving heart with his love for hats to bless others and provide encouragement. We were able to serve the community for the first time on Veteran's Day 2019. We were invited to the local Veterans Center and they had a veteran's celebration and appreciation. I was able to share my story about Anthony, his service, and his life and gave over 100 veterans' hats and motivational bracelets to all the veterans that were in attendance. It was a beautiful program, and I was able to honor the memory of my son in a healthy way.

There is hope for positive impact as a result of grief and pain; it can be rewarding. There is power in pain. This foundation was one way of bridging my grief to something that would have a positive impact on others. It is the means by which he will never die again. The veterans were humbled that I would take the time to celebrate them for their service, but I quickly told them that the pleasure is mine. It gives me pleasure to see the faces of the veterans and their families, the way that I get to tell them about Anthony and how he proudly served his country, but mostly his name and legacy of giving will continue to live through this wonderful work.

The key is to not sweep the pain of grief under the rug. Do not pretend that it is not happening. Do not allow it to traumatize you to be inactive. Do not allow others to rush your process. Give healthy language to your hurt and pain. Prayer helps you to breakthrough to a place of victory and joy. You have to build yourself up before the crisis so that you will be able to stand when the hard times comes. It will not be a perfect journey, but our weaknesses are made perfect in God through His Word and prayer. Ultimately, we must remember

It's Ok to Cry

that we will all go through some type of loss in our lives; whether it's losing a loved one, losing a marriage, losing a job, losing your home, or being estranged from your family. It all brings grief. Just remember that it is okay to cry! Let the tears cleanse your heart and soul so that you can continue to live in joy and peace. It is okay to cry! It's okay to cry!

A Prayer For You

Heavenly Father, I thank you for all who have read this book. I pray that my testimony is encouragement that what You have done before, You will do it again. I pray that everyone receive these prayer strategies for their own life and continue to press through this time of loss and grief.

Lord, You are close to the brokenhearted and bind up every wound; And I thank You now for healing our heart today. We receive Your perfect peace that transcends all knowledge and understanding. I pray that our heart will not be consumed with sorrow but remain in Your presence where there is fullness of joy. I thank You that we do not have to be afraid or worry and that we can come to You with confidence and boldness. I thank You that You have touched every heart and continue to love us as no one else can. I pray now that anxiety, depression, worry and fear be torn from our life and that peace, joy, faith, and love will always abide in us. We trust You God, even when we don't understand. We commit our life into Your hands and thank You in advance for the great things that You will do in and through us. Thank You God, for being such an awesome Father. You are the One who we can count on to fight all of our battles. You are the One who heals and provides. You are the One who gives us grace and mercy. We exalt and bless Your Name. We give You all of the honor, glory, and praise. In the name of Jesus Christ, Amen.

Scriptures to Help You on Your Journey of Breakthrough

Those who mourn are blessed, for they will be comforted. Matthew 5:4 HCSB

Let your steadfast love comfort me according to your promise to your servant. Psalm 119:76 ESV

The LORD is near to the brokenhearted and saves the crushed in spirit. Psalm 34:18 ESV

I will rejoice and be glad in your steadfast love, because you have seen my affliction; you have known the distress of my soul. Psalm 31:7 ESV

In my distress I called to the LORD, and He answered me. Psalm 120:1 ESV

Be gracious to me, O LORD, for I am in distress; my eye is wasted from grief; my soul and my body also. Psalm 31:9 ESV

It's Ok to Cry

So be truly glad. There is wonderful joy ahead, even though you have to endure many trials for a little while. I Peter 1:5&6 NLT

He will wipe every tear from their eyes. There will be no more death or mourning or crying or pain, for the old order of things has passed away. Revelation 21:4 NIV

So also you have sorrow now, but I will see you again, and your hearts will rejoice, and no one will take your joy from you. John 16:20-22 ESV

So be strong and courageous! Do not be afraid and do not panic before them. For the LORD your God will personally go ahead of you. He will neither fail you nor abandon you. Deuteronomy 31:6 NLT

You will be delivered by returning and resting; your strength will lie in quiet confidence. Isaiah 30:15 HCSB

"For the mountains may depart and the hills be removed, but my steadfast love shall not depart from you, and my covenant of peace shall not be removed," says the LORD, who has compassion on you. Isaiah 54:10 ESV

Princess S. Millens

This is my comfort in my affliction, that your promise gives me life. Psalm 119:153 ESV

Hear my prayer, LORD, and listen to my cry for help; do not be silent at my tears. For I am a foreigner residing with You, a temporary resident like all my fathers. Psalm 39:12 HCSB

About The Author

Mother – Teacher – Author – Entrepreneur – Servant of God

Princess S. Millens is a native of Atlanta, GA. She is the founder of Blessed and Beautiful International, an organization dedicated to serving women worldwide and help them to become healthy in all areas of life. She is also the founder of MBS Ministries, a nonprofit organization that serves the elderly and disabled as well as Next Generation Legacy, Inc that serves youth. Anthony's Army is a foundation established by Princess in honor and memory of her son who proudly served the US Army, which honors veterans with hats and other motivational products. Princess is a mathematics educator. She is the proud mother of DeAndrea, Ayanna, and Anthony. She loves God and His Word and committed to serving people in need.

Printed in Great Britain
by Amazon